CELEBRATE EACH STEP

BUILD YOUR BUSINESS AND YOUR LIFE BY
MASTERING THE TOOLS OF CELEBRATION

Tommie Jean Valmassy

D1490248

Tommie Jean Valmassy
100 Little River Ct. #7
Vallejo, CA 94591

Celebrate Each Step: Build Your Business and Your Live by Mastering the Tools of Celebration/ Tommie Jean Valmassy —1st ed.
ISBN 979-8-218-03803-8

Table of Contents

For my daughter, Magnolia. The day you entered the world was the happiest day of my life. You are so joyful, and every day with you is a reason to celebrate. Love you, Mom

INTRODUCTION

"People change best by feeling good, not by feeling bad." BJ Fogg, PhD

I awoke from a dream with an overwhelming feeling of peace and joy. I sat up at 6:30 a.m. one day in 2018 and knew the purpose of life. Or, at least, the purpose of my life. Joyfully Create. That's it, that is all I recalled when I awoke. But I felt so certain and peaceful.

That peaceful feeling stayed with me through the day. At some point I thought "create what, though?" I spent the next few years seeking an answer to what I am supposed to create. I'm not an artist or a woodworker. I wondered if I'm supposed to create books since I like to write. Or learn something new and use that skill to create. Finally, I figured out my answer. My purpose is to joyfully create my own life. That's it; it's that simple and that hard.

I had never had a dream like that before, and I haven't had one since. I know it sounds kind of "woo woo." But I've learned that if we pay attention we all have dreams, or instincts, or gut feelings that lead us in the right direction, or away from the wrong one.

Creating my own life sometimes feels like a lot of responsibility. And sometimes it feels like a lot of people and things are in the way. Now that I use celebration to build the life and business I want, I am joyfully creating my life, including my business.

This book offers these ideas:

- Building a business, and a life, requires a lot of action.
- People are able to take consistent action by feeling good rather than feeling bad.
- Small steps can lead to massive things, but only if you can keep going with those small steps.
- The way to keep going is to celebrate.
- There are more ways to celebrate than you might think, and you can build a toolbox of celebration so you're ready when awesome things happen.

What is your overall strategy in business and in life; do you have one? Yah, I didn't either. Through experience, my winning strategy is, simply: celebrate each step. You DO NOT NEED permission, approval, or even support. Celebrate each step forward.

This book is all about self-celebration. While I share some ideas about how to celebrate with others, you don't need to rely on someone else to tell you whether what you did is worth celebrating, how to celebrate it, or even to celebrate with you. Can I get a "hell yeah!"?

CHAPTER ONE – IF BEATING YOURSELF UP DOESN'T WORK

I paid good money to be yelled at. Well, technically I was paying for a monthly gym membership, and the class was optional, but I was still paying for it. I don't remember the exact name of the class, but it had "Bootcamp" in the title. It was very popular, always full, and I was excited to join in. That excitement didn't last long.

Everything in this class was a race. All of the bootcampers had to get from one side of the room to the other by running, running backwards, jumping, high kicking, and so on, back and forth. Those who finished first would stand and watch those of us still slogging across the floor and the instructor just kept yelling "let's go, let's go!" At one point, we had to crab walk across the room. If you can't picture that exercise, look it up. It was gross. My hands were touching the ground that all these people were walking across, my sideways movement was slow, and I was still in the middle of the room while most people were done.

I was encouraged with a collective glare of impatience and more yelling from the instructor. This was 15 years ago, and I still remember that feeling. Being yelled at and trying to keep going while being hit with a laser focus of disgust did not help me get better results.

Yet for many years I kept up with activities that required me to compare myself to others rather than to my own progress and goals. I kept spending time with people who told me I wasn't enough. Worst of all, my only method for encouraging myself to do something was to mentally beat myself up.

Are you your own worst critic? You miss the mark with something and you don't need anyone to tell you that you messed up. They can't make you feel worse than the mean voice in your head is making you feel.

Many men say that what they do wrong is what is most often pointed out. I've heard men say they feel they could do 100 things right, and the one thing they do "wrong" is the focus. If you've ever felt that way, I say: no more!

Often women seem to be their own toughest critics, automatically focusing on the next thing to be done, on the undone, on the imperfectly done, until they just feel done. No more of that, either!

The good news? If you feel that way, criticized by others or by yourself, you can change it. In fact, you are the only one who can change it. That's right, you can change the feelings of being criticized by others and by yourself, all on your own. With a little help from this book.

Just Getting Through It
I had a client, Jim, who was rushing through phone calls with clients. He had a backlog of calls to return and he felt like he had to get through the list of calls as soon as possible. He started every call with an apology for the wait and then rushed people. He was beating himself up, figuratively, for not being able to return calls faster and for not making more sales. It wasn't the positive client experience he wanted to give, and he never felt good when the list was complete, even though completing the list was the goal.

Jim realized that completing the list wasn't really the right goal for his business. Instead, Jim focused on connecting with each person he spoke to. He began calls by thanking people for waiting and letting them know they had his full attention. By doing this, Jim was able to really listen to each client and make a stronger connection. The calls didn't really take much longer and he began celebrating each time he connected and helped a client, instead of just slogging through a list.

Sometimes approaching a task with an attitude to just get through it is a way of beating yourself up. Instead of a goal to make as many calls as possible, Jim set himself up for success by setting a goal of connecting during each call. And he celebrated each connection using some tools from his own celebration toolkit.

Providing a pleasing reward to encourage a behavior that you want repeated can be much more effective than punishing yourself. The term in psychology is Positive Reinforcement. Note that I am not a psychologist and this is not a psychology book. However, this book is about you as an individual, how you can explore your own mindset when it comes to building your business and your life. You'll also find your own ways to celebrate so you get that positive reinforcement that we all need.

Celebration is the opposite of criticism AND you can celebrate all on your own, in a way that truly feels good to you.

If you have beat yourself up, compared your progress to others, approached your days just trying to get through them, denied yourself joy, leisure, and satisfaction, or just been your own bully, there is a different, more effective, more joyful way.

CHAPTER TWO – EXACTLY WHAT SHOULD I CELEBRATE?

"Most people tell you there are certain moments you should celebrate in life: for example, the weekend coming, so you should party on a Friday. Or your birthday or New Year's Eve. But what if you're excited about being alive every day? Can't you be in that celebratory state every moment you're not dead?" Andrew W.K., musician

Today my coach asked me what I wanted to celebrate from the previous week. I went on about some of the work I've been putting in, my recent consistency, a new way of doing things. But what I really wanted to celebrate was the fact that I took care of the numerous bridge toll invoices and violations that I'd stacked up in the past few months.

I live near a bay and cross bridges all the time. And it ain't free! In my divorce I guess I lost custody of the electronic toll device. I tried to go on-line and open my own account but ran into technical difficulty that required me to call a government office. I tried one whole time. There was a 43-minute wait. I hung up and started accruing late fees instead.

I know a particular businesswoman who runs a 7-figure company and helps hundreds of women reach their goals each year. She admitted that she had let her driver's license expire. It took her months to get it renewed. And I'm sure she was driving during that time.

Another amazing entrepreneur who is a creative genius and employs a full team had to get the electricity turned back on at her studio because she kept forgetting to pay that bill. Why not set it to be paid automatically, we asked. She just didn't get around to it. Yep, I get that.

Here is what I learned from the expired licensee and the dark studio owner: **oh well**. They both did a forehead smack and acknowledged they should figure this out. And eventually they did figure it out. But they didn't make it define WHO they are. They didn't participate in self talk about being bad or stupid or lazy or any of the other things I often used to say to myself when I made a big, impatient error in judgement. I should have taken care of that electronic toll issue much sooner. But I didn't. So when I finally did, I celebrated.

Maybe you would never accrue fines or have the lights turned off. But maybe you wait until a client asks you for what you were supposed to deliver before you work on it. Or maybe you don't invoice for a few months. Maybe you know the campground your family loves will book up, but you still don't book early. I know some people who just cannot return library books, get gas before their tank is empty, or file their taxes without an extension. Good people, smart people, "together" kind of people. Because really, nobody is together in every aspect.

One of the best ways to deal with those things we put off is to celebrate. Some things you can take off of your to-do list, but some you have to do, and you can't delegate them. So celebrate the fact that you called the DMV to make an appointment, or the fact that you at least gathered your tax paperwork. Maybe you can delegate, then celebrate taking a small step to hire an assistant who will track your invoicing or set up on-line payment for your utility bills.

Yes, you were supposed to do it a long time ago. That's not a helpful thing to say to yourself. And it won't help you the next time you procrastinate. Celebrating and acknowledging things you've done, even if you are supposed to do them, feels good. Here is what you may need to hear: You deserve to feel good. You deserve to make things a little easier on yourself. If beating yourself up, being critical, and always pointing out what you've done wrong truly works for you, keep doing that. But if you're like a lot of people, feeling bad, unmotivated, and overwhelmed, try feeling good about what you do. How? By celebrating it.

Doing What You Are Supposed to Do

My client Andy was making steady progress with his goal of daily reading. He went from rarely doing his morning reading to doing it 4-5 times a week. His response when I pointed that out: "Yah, I just can't seem to do more than that." Hold up, you went from ZERO to at least 4. That's great. You don't have to get to the goal to feel pleased with progress. I suggested Andy celebrate each time he did his morning reading. He balked. No way. Too much.

OK, instead of using "celebrate" how about acknowledge. Note each time you read and say "Yes, I did it another day!"

Andy warmed up to the idea of acknowledging the steps he was taking, but then confessed that he didn't think he should celebrate or acknowledge something he is SUPPOSED to do.

Ah-ha. There was no way for Andy to win and feel good. Anything he did was just a thing he was supposed to be doing already. And anything short of the larger goal was failing. And if you're going to fail, then why try...

I asked Andy if he says thank you when a waiter brings his meal. "Yes, of course."
"But why? They are SUPPOSED to bring your meal."
"Yes" he said, "but they deserve kindness and to be acknowledged..."
Lightbulb!

If a stranger at a restaurant deserves gratitude, kindness, and to be acknowledged for doing their job (and can we all just agree that yes, they do deserve that) then why can't we give ourselves acknowledgement when we do something we are SUPPOSED to do? Andy still doesn't always call it celebration, and that's OK. For him, it's acknowledgement.

So, what should you celebrate? That thing you did, that step you took, that progress you made.

Focusing on things we can control leads to much greater achievement and satisfaction than focusing on things we cannot control. That's why it's helpful to celebrate the thing you did, rather than the result.

For example, you could say you are going to celebrate when you get 1,000 followers on the social media account for your business. That might not be within your immediate control. But you can celebrate when you post five days in a row, or when your stats show increased engagement, all leading to more followers.

I used to think about celebration as synonymous with popping champagne, elaborate dinners, or parades. Those are all great, but we can celebrate in hundreds of different ways, elaborate to tiny. Our brains are wired for reward and celebration.

Hiding Our Achievements

My friend, I'll call her Jenna, wrote a book. A book! Wrote it, designed the cover, and published it. It was a huge life goal, and a topic very special to her. That sounds like the kind of goal worth popping champagne over. Or at least announcing. She did neither. Instead, she became afraid that people would not like the book, that family members would not like what she wrote, or that sharing her book was imposing on others. What the hell, Jenna? You need to celebrate! In fact, Jenna is one of the people who inspired me to write this book.

I have a client who is the only businessman in his family. When he expanded his business, he kept quiet about it. He didn't want to brag or make family members feel uncomfortable. Let's face it, family members mean well but they can be tough. That's why it's OK to celebrate alone, or to find people who are like-minded and share your achievements with them. Just not celebrating, however, is not the best bet for continuing to move forward.

Putting the 'Fun' in Fundamental

Humans usually know what we need to do. Sleep enough. Drink water. Save 10% off the top. Move our bodies. We need to master the fundamentals. YAWN. That is so boring. Nobody wants to hear that.

If you ask any great athletic coach, they will say the best players master the fundamentals. It's not just sinking a basket, it's sinking it repeatedly, 100 times in a row. Master the run, the throw, the swing, the catch, in any sport. Focus on the fundamentals; there is no shortcut.

There may be no shortcut, but there is a hack. If the way to success is to master the fundamentals, the way to keep going with the fundamentals is to celebrate when you do them. I think you knew I was going to say that.

What are the fundamentals in your business? In Chapter 3 we'll talk about finding those fundamentals and allowing them to help you build your business, step-by-step, celebrating along the way.

CHAPTER THREE - HOW WILL CELEBRATION BUILD MY BUSINESS?

"Celebrate what you want to see more of."
Tom Peters, best-selling business author

I n chapter 2 I talked about mastering the fundamentals. Our human bodies all have similar fundamental physical and emotional needs, though they vary. Some of us need more sleep, some of us need to include or avoid different foods, etc. I wrote this book for a lot of reasons. One group I really want to help is my coaching clients. Small business owners, entrepreneurs, people who work on commission and are motivated to create a thriving business.

Your business has fundamentals, too. They may be the same as many other businesses, generally, but your requirements vary slightly.

The fundamentals are what keep your business **alive, healthy, and functioning**. The basics usually include sales - a certain amount of revenue coming in. It also includes staff, whether that be just you or maybe you also have employees. And it usually includes systems. A system for getting clients, a system for serving them, a system for ensuring quality, a system for training people, a system for collecting payment, etc.

Celebrating small steps will help you build your business in a multitude of ways. The three primary ones are:

1. Help you break things into smaller steps
2. Motivate you to keep moving forward
3. Prevent burnout

Break Things Into Smaller Steps
A marathon is 26.2 miles. That's really far. You could run one mile and think "Oh man, I still have more than 25 to go." Or you could think "Yes, one mile down already!" Which one do you think helps your mindset get to the finish line? Breaking a marathon into smaller steps and milestones is key to finishing.

"What I think a lot of great marathon runners do is envision crossing that finish line. Visualization is critical. But for me, I set a lot of little goals along the way to get my mind off that overwhelming goal of 26.2 miles. I know I've got to get to 5, and 12, and 16, and then I celebrate those little victories along the way." - Bill Rancic, entrepreneur

Keep Moving Forward

Are you familiar with the movie The Shawshank Redemption? The protagonist, Andy, dug his way out of prison with a tiny rock hammer. It took 19 years. Talk about daunting. There's no way he could have kept going if he didn't find some sort of satisfaction, a mini celebration, in each pebble he hammered away.

This is an extreme example. It's relevant because if a wrongly incarcerated man can find the mental strength to chip away for 19 years all while risking being caught, then maybe you and I can offer our products and services repeatedly even though we may get a no. You and I can keep trying to hire someone who is truly a help in our business even though hiring is frustrating and training new staff takes so much time. I can keep putting words on a page until I finish this book. You can keep networking even though interest rates are high and it feels like no one is buying. Celebration keeps you moving forward.

Prevent Burnout

Burnout is working at an unsustainable pace for an unsustainable time. When you celebrate each small step, you are allowing your best effort to be enough.

Thinking of the marathon example above, building and running a business is definitely more of a marathon than a sprint. If you don't celebrate each mile(stone) discouragement can set in quickly. Can we agree that burnout and being super busy is not a requirement to be in business?

By breaking things into smaller steps you can focus on just the step in front of you. It is also true that many of the items on your to-do list are not vital, necessary, or truly productive. That's difficult to hear, but it's true. If you keep the bigger objective in mind, you can notice whether the steps you are taking are the most vital, or if you are just side-stepping the truly important tasks.

I've heard that baking fresh cookies during an open house can help a home sell for more. That may be true. But if you are a realtor and your ultimate goal is to sell the house, there are probably a lot more important small steps. Perhaps it's staging the house, setting an appropriate price, holding an open house or realtor tour. What if making the cookies is something you like to do? Don't fool yourself into thinking it's a vital step. Do the truly vital steps first and celebrate each of those steps. The celebration is meant to make those vital steps more rewarding and fun. Then maybe you will have the energy to make the cookies, knowing it's an extra. Sometimes you have to reject the cookies.

Another common example I have heard is spending hours and hours on a newsletter to send to clients. A business owner may include the latest industry news, tips, articles about events, and consider this vital work to keep in touch.

Keeping in touch may be vital. But is a labor-intensive newsletter more effective than picking up the phone? Placing a small ad? Attending a networking event? You can still send a newsletter, but maybe you don't need to spend 20 hours considering font, writing new materials to fill 4 pages, and searching for clever Churchill quotes that fit in perfectly with your carpet cleaning, insurance, or social media marketing business.

These extra steps contribute to burnout in a big way. They feel good because they are enjoyable and it seems like you're working on your business. However, there may be tasks like this that do not lead to results. Instead, celebrate the small steps, especially the difficult or annoying things you must do to get results. These are examples; if homemade cookies or an elaborate newsletter are part of your effective business fundamentals, then continue. It's important to figure out what your fundamentals really are.

There's a bonus way that celebration can help you build your business: it makes you more enjoyable to be around. Have you ever just felt that someone was insincere, going through the motions, or feeling burned out? It's an icky feeling that repels. Have you ever felt it when someone has good energy, is genuinely happy and a pleasure to be around? What if their secret is that they celebrate each step they take? Do you enjoy being "around" yourself? What if celebrating those small steps makes you enjoy your own company more?

Take a moment now to consider the fundamentals of your business. Remember, it's the eat/sleep/move type fundamentals.

The fundamentals of my business include:

Do you track the fundamentals you listed? If you want to sleep enough or drink enough water, often you have to start by measuring what you're doing. What do you need to track better?

Remember the example of mastering the fundamentals in sports and think of sinking the shot 100 times in a row. Is there a fundamental above that you need to practice so when you get your shot, you're making it?

Are you annoyed or discouraged because you struggled with the list above? That's OK, I struggled with it, too. The good news is now you can think about what the fundamentals of your business are and then start mastering them.

Celebrate this opportunity to learn something new.

CHAPTER FOUR – WHAT COUNTS AS A CELEBRATION?

The man and the woman were strangers. They had never seen each other before and would never see each other again after this night. But for a brief moment, their bodies reacted simultaneously. They both shouted "Yes!" Their hands came together, and with wild abandon... they high fived each other as the batter rounded the bases, and their team was headed to the playoffs.

Have you ever high fived a stranger at a ballgame, when your team scores? Well, I have. When I think about it, it's kind of silly. And yet, it's amazingly fun. That is a celebration.

It can be easy for us to celebrate with our friends, to celebrate our team, to get in on the excitement around us. But what if you could bring that high-five, hell yes feeling to something you did?

For something to count as a celebration (according to me, the self-appointed Queen of Celebration) it has to be:
- Deliberate – you do it with the intent to celebrate;

- Immediate – as soon as possible when your step is complete
- Pleasurable – it should feel good on a physical or emotional level.

My friend Stacey loves acronyms. So, for this, remember DIP. Deliberate, immediate, pleasurable. As you read on, you'll find all sorts of ways to celebrate.

Celebrations, Rewards, and Simple Rights
I think it's important to talk about the difference between a celebration, a reward, and a simple right.

Celebration is acknowledgement. Anything that positively acknowledges that thing you did is a celebration.

Reward is often a thing. A ribbon, a certificate, money, goods. It's about stuff. And while stuff can be great, for the purpose of this book, celebration is a verb, not a noun. (There are plenty of people who disagree with me about this and talk about activating the reward center of your brain. For the purpose of this book, a reward is a thing, and most of us are looking for fewer things in our lives.) However, you will also find several examples of a thing you can buy or get to celebrate in this book. That's just not the primary focus.

Simple Rights are things you deserve. You deserve pleasure, joy, and relaxation on a regular basis. Please do not start withholding things you already like to do and then calling them celebrations.

The purpose of this book is to encourage you to notice and acknowledge your progress and general awesomeness. You can't do that if you are withholding from yourself. For example, if you enjoy a gooey, peanut butter and syrup covered waffle every Friday morning before work (a real example from a family member), don't suddenly put requirements around it, such as you only get it if you finish a certain task. You are awesome, and if a Friday waffle is a simple pleasure, please keep it. Now, if you don't often let yourself have that waffle or just usually forget to make one, you can plan that as a celebration.

One client of mine loves a scalding hot bath with a cold beer or a bit of whiskey. But it's difficult to make time for that. So he will use it as a celebration that also relaxes his body and releases muscle tension. It's a physical celebration. Again, if you take a hot steamy bath regularly, don't start withholding it and making yourself have to earn it now.

A celebration can be huge, explosive, amazing, like fireworks. Or a celebration can be simple, easy, and found in your pocket, like a piece of gum.

To count as a celebration, as noted above, it has to be deliberate, immediate, and pleasurable. Those three things.

Let's say you want to exercise more. Maybe in the past you would have told yourself you are a lazy, fat f*ck who needs to get it together, then gone on a punishing 5-mile run, hurt your knee, and stopped all exercise for the next two weeks. Yikes.

Or maybe you outlined a full plan: sign up for a pricey gym membership, start waking up at 5am and workout 1 hour each day at least 5 days a week. That can be a good goal, but not a first step. If you just aim for the big goal and you miss it, you're building up evidence of failure. Set up smaller goals and celebrate them.

What is the first step? Is it signing up at the gym? Is it waking up at 5am one time and taking a quick walk outside? If you want to work out 5 times a week, start with one. Celebrate the one. If you want to increase sales by networking, choose the smallest step, maybe making one phone call, and celebrate that call, regardless of the outcome. If you are trying to build a habit or get to a certain big goal, celebrate each step along the way.

My friend Nichole wants to be stronger so she can be better at surfing, and so she can pick up her two little girls, who grow taller and heavier each day. She joined a gym, and her goal is to do one pull-up within the year. The fact is, she's not even close. If she only measured success as being able to do the pull-up she would be discouraged. Instead, she celebrates each time she goes to the gym, and she's building strength. This doesn't mean that her celebration is a cookie or popping champagne every time she goes to the gym.

Often, it's looking at her gym tracker app and noticing how many times she been to the gym. Or it's texting a friend to say that she went. Or it's a fist pump and a flex. Those all count as celebrations because they are deliberate, they are immediate, and they bring her pleasure.

My client Gerry was struggling to hire and keep good employees for his small business. In fact, he realized that he was turning customers away because he didn't have staff availability. This realization made him focus on the business fundamental of hiring. The simple ad on one job board wasn't enough. I suggested (demanded) he make a list of 100 ways to hire.

It took Gerry 3 hours to make the list. He ran out of ideas at number 30. Then more popped into his head. He let some ideas be silly, like getting a tattoo that reads, "we're hiring." But it kept his brain thinking creatively, and it became fun. List item number 83 became the first one he implemented. If he had stopped at 30, or even 75, he wouldn't have found this idea.

Each idea added to the list felt good. Gerry celebrated just finishing the list. Then he was excited to try his hiring idea, knowing he had a lot of options he could try later. If Gerry could only feel good once he had hired, trained, and retained 5 new employees, then imagine the ongoing frustration and defeat.

Do you remember the modern stone age family? Each day when the dinosaur whistle blew, Fred

Flintstone would yell "Yabba Dabba Doo!" and head home to Wilma and Pebbles. That's a celebration. Whether you watch the clock to know when you're done for the day or end the day by completing a task or appeasing a boss or customer, being done for the day is awesome. Honestly, if you're loving your business, then starting your day can also feel fantastic. Yabba Dabba Doo it. You can literally yell that phrase or come up with your own. A good fist pump also goes a long way in letting your body and mind know that you are celebrating whether it be the start or the end of the day.

I've said you can and should celebrate on your own, meaning you don't need to wait for someone to celebrate with you, to tell you you're worthy of celebration, or to throw you a party. It's like having a workout buddy. It's great if you have one. But you have to keep going with your own exercise goals and practices whether your buddy shows up or not.

In the next chapter you'll get some ideas about celebrations to try so you can build your own celebration toolkit.

CHAPTER FIVE – CREATE YOUR CELEBRATION TOOLKIT

L ike any good scout, it's important to be prepared. If you plan to eat more healthfully you have to buy healthy food. If you want to sell more products you have to have products to sell. If you are going to celebrate, you have to be ready.

Planning celebrations ahead of time is a great way to keep yourself motivated. After you plan WHAT steps you will celebrate you can plan HOW you will celebrate those steps.

It can be hard to find ways to celebrate if you are only used to celebrating huge milestones. See chapter 6 for a bunch of ideas if you want inspiration. But I suggest starting by picking a few things in each of the five categories below. Have them ready for the next time you're going to celebrate that step you took. None of these are things you have to buy, just plan to do a few of them.

The Stance: I mean the way in which a person stands. (If you are unable to stand, some of these will still work for you.) Adopt a celebratory stance. There's the superhero (legs apart, fists on hips, chin lifted, imaginary cape blowing behind you) the bodybuilder (flexed muscles), the champion (one arm in the air like you won a boxing match). Or maybe it's a fist pump, or both arms in the air. You can even yell "I'm the King of the World" a la Leonardo in Titanic. Pick a stance and practice it.

The Savor: In this instance I define savor as "to enjoy completely". This can be something you already do, but instead you will savor it. Food and drink come to mind, such as the first sip of cool water or hot coffee. It can also be savoring your shower and the smell of your soap, savoring the feeling of your head hitting the pillow, or relaxing into a big hug from your spouse. Decide what you want to truly savor.

The Share: Feeling like we need approval to celebrate can be a stumbling block. But often people want to celebrate with us. Sharing means telling someone that step you took. The best ways to share are not dependent upon likes or shares or retweets to validate it.

It can be a text with happy emojis, or a shared white board in the office. Think of those goal thermometer signs. Set a goal and fill in the red on the thermometer until you get there. When people see what the goal is they may cheer you on or contribute to make the red go up to the top.

You could also share with a kid or a dog. They are pretty good at a paw shake or high-five, even if they don't know why. Celebrate with one of those.

The Silly: By silly, I mean playful. Blow a noisemaker. Wear all green every Monday because you've got your money on your mind. See if you can still do the worm or the running man. I recently saw a man driving a beautiful, luxurious sports car - with a red clown nose on the front. He's having fun and not taking it too seriously.

For several years I rode the ferry across the bay into San Francisco to get to and from work. Every Friday afternoon a woman with long, black hair would play a song called Aloha Friday as the ferry pulled away. It was her weekly celebration, and she was sharing it with us.

The Sublime: I'm using this synonymously with awe-inspiring, divine, glorious. Some things are nice, fun, good. Here we are after the pinnacle, the sublime.

This can refer to opening that 60-year-old whiskey, listening to a concerto that gives you goosebumps, eating not just a piece of grocery-store cake, but a hand-crafted specialty cupcake that tastes so good you want to rub it on your face. This isn't the massage chair at the mall, it's the deep tissue, full hour, muscles are liquid feeling from the spa.

Do any of these ideas sound fun to you? Remember the key to a good celebration is that it brings YOU pleasure.

If you are ready to brainstorm more ideas personal to you and your best way to celebrate, here are some questions to ask yourself:

10 Questions to Help You Build Your Celebration Toolkit

1. What was the first, or best, concert you've ever been to? Play a song from that artist/band and revel in the memory. Write down a memory about it. Put on the concert t-shirt if you still have it. See if they still tour and buy tickets.

2. What is your favorite animal? Find a video or photos on-line of that animal. You can search for live webcams at nature preserves, funny cat videos, talking dogs, or even look up sea turtles. Whatever you like.

3. What was your favorite game as a child? How can you do it now? Play Candyland or Monopoly virtually on-line. Go to a park and bounce a ball against a backstop. Start impromptu charades after dinner tonight.

4. What is your favorite part of your body? Do something fun with it or nice for it. If you like your arms - flex them. If you like your hands - nourish them with lotion. Got beautiful eyes - take a selfie of just your eyes. Love your pretty tummy - bang it like a drum. Whatever feels fun. No one has to know.

5. What is your dream vacation? Pretend you are there. Do you dream of a tropical vacation?

Eat some pineapple and play the sound of waves. Do you wish you were in Manhattan? Eat a bagel and look at pictures of your favorite skyscrapers. Yearn for Spain? Play some Spanish music and have Sangria.

6. Who do you love? Look at a photo of your sweet grandchild. Call your spouse. Write a fan letter to a celebrity. Tell your dog he's a goodboy.

7. Who keeps trying to help you? Let them. Does the grocery store offer to take your groceries to the car? Say yes. Does your aunt offer to babysit? Say yes. Does your neighbor ask if you want anything from the coffee shop? Say yes. Who keeps leaving a landscaping flier on your door? Let them take care of your yard. Does your coach ask how she can support you this week? Tell her what you need. And celebrate your luck of having this help.

8. Do you prefer to be hot or cold? Get that way. If cold is your preference, drink a frozen beverage, put ice on your head, turn on a fan. If you prefer to be warm, put on a cozy hoodie and slippers, light a fire, plug in a heating pad.

9. What good stuff are you saving? Use it now. Use the soft guest towels, the wedding china, the new shampoo even though some is left in the old bottle. Wear cologne for no reason, use the expensive coffee grounds you save for guests, wear the fancy watch or the sentimental necklace. Enjoy.

10. What would you buy a teenager if you had to get them the coolest gift ever right now? Maybe you should get it for yourself. You are

a grown up and can do what you want. Buy that hoverboard for yourself. Get some virtual reality goggles, tickets to the music festival, or the latest iPhone. Be the cool aunt or uncle to yourself.

Some ideas for my celebrations:

CHAPTER SIX – 10 WAYS TO CELEBRATE...

Remember the important rules for building your business and your life with celebration: (1) It should be deliberate, with the intention of celebrating. (2) It should be done almost immediately. (3) It should be pleasurable to you. Some of these may not seem like they can be done immediately. They can if you prepare a little and know how you are going to celebrate. Have it ready in advance if you can. And really, savor whatever you choose.

10 Ways to Celebrate for $5 or Less

1. Gum. I don't mean the small, sharply minty kind you keep in the car for after you've had coffee. I mean some flavor, something you can blow a bubble with. Most mini marts and gas stations still sell Hubba Bubba, Fruit Stripe, and Big Red. Even the fanciest gum is less than $5.
2. Upgrade your coffee order. Add flavored syrup or steamed milk. If that's not your style, get an extra shot of espresso, add cinnamon, try that pink drink everyone seems to love, or just get a bigger size.
3. Buy a luscious fruit or vegetable. Sometimes produce is so expensive I find myself buying cheap tomatoes. But I could splurge on one of those juicy, strangely-hued heirlooms for less than 5 bucks. Slice and devour with some salt and/or oil. Heavenly! (Some of you hate tomatoes and just barfed a little. Maybe a juicy peach, ripe berries, or a perfect squash?)
4. Whipped cream. Add some to your breakfast, your dessert, or just spray it in your mouth. Give some to your pup, too.
5. "Hidden Google Games." Search this and have fun playing games on Google. My favorite is Atari Breakout. This option is actually FREE.
6. Play-doh. You can buy one small tub in just about any color. It's fun to have at your desk to squeeze, squish, and even smell.
7. Give someone $5. It's not a lot, but wouldn't you feel great if you got that? It can be a fiver

in a tip jar, a $5 gift card to your neighbor for no reason, $5 in a card to a distant niece or nephew. Your joy will expand when they receive it.

8. Experiment with art supplies. Spend $5 at the Dollar Store, or whatever equivalent you have nearby, on art supplies. You can get paper, pens, stickers, markers, paint, yarn, ribbon, fake flowers. Pick a few items and make something.

9. Don't drink from the can. Buy yourself a beer, sparkling water, tea, cold brew, or any of the thousands of canned drinks available. Then pour it in a chilled stein, wine glass, or favorite mug. I'm doing it while I type this.

10. Buy an app. Instead of the free version with ads, spend $1.99 and upgrade to the ad-free version. Ooh, now that is luxury.

10 Ways to Celebrate That Aren't Food

Of course, it's OK to celebrate with food. But that's typically the easiest, most common way most of us celebrate. Here are some ideas to get you thinking outside the fridge.

1. Follow something you already love on social media. We talk a lot about removing negative things from our social media, and that's effective self-care. But you can also add in a lot of joy. Check out the feeds of your favorite band, the town you grew up in, a magician, a BMX pro, an athlete or team, an author you admire now or loved as a kid, a farm or zoo. There are some really great things people are sharing.
2. Play music. Your celebration tunes may be arena rock, country, hip hop, doo-wop, or maybe just a jingle you can't get out of your head. Singing along is a must, and dancing along is better. Create a celebration playlist.
3. Write in a nice journal. I bought one of my clients a simple, leather journal that he enjoys writing in. When tracking his health metrics, he writes them in that leather journal, enjoying the smell and feel. And he gives himself a star by the things he is doing well.
4. Call a cleaning service. Have them come clean your house top to bottom. Here is the wild part: don't pre-clean before they come.
5. Get your car detailed. You probably spend a lot of time in your car. Get the new car smell,

or whatever smell you like. Notice how big the sky is now that the windshield is spotless. Marvel at the way they got that sticky spot off the throw mat. You can enjoy this for days or weeks.

6. Buy a lottery ticket. Whether it's been a day or a decade since you've thought about the lottery, give yourself the fun of imagining a win.

7. Light a candle. You can get a cheap but fragrant one at the grocery store. Or you can order one that smells like the ocean, like leather, like certain states, flowers, seasons.

8. Do something you're good at. I recently learned to crack an egg with one hand. I'm not winning a talent contest with that, but I get excited when I crack an egg now. Maybe you have a cool way to lace your shoes, shuffle cards, tie a tie, slice a pie, skip a rock, fold a sock. Do your special little skill just for you.

9. Buy something fun and joyful related to your goals. Eating plant-based: subscribe to a month of vegetarian meal boxes. Working out more: buy those thick, supportive socks. Want to talk about your business more: order some custom business cards and matching pens. Again, it just has to be pleasurable to YOU.

10. Blow something up, celebration style. Fireworks are illegal where I live. But tossing mentos into a 2-liter of diet coke (outside on the lawn) is legal and pretty fun. So is popping bubble wrap or a balloon filled with shaving cream.

10 Ways to Celebrate at the Office

You may have an office shared with others, a home office, a laptop and a van, or a storefront. You have some place of work, even if it moves or doubles as the dining room. Here are some ways to celebrate at whatever place you call your office.

1. Announce a milestone. If you've been in business for a while, let people know. Post a sign, change your zoom background, and add it to your email signature: celebrating 10 years in business. It can be one year, 7 years, 6 months, any number.
2. Use post-its. I had a client who was losing sleep at night because she kept forgetting to add key information into the customer management database. She used a post-it to remind herself and included a funny little face on it. The post-it made her smile every day and adding the information became a happy habit.
3. Read positive feedback. I have an email folder called "feedback" though I only put positive feedback in it. Every year I look over any email I got that made me feel appreciated. You can do this with emails, post-it notes you've received, saved texts, etc. Find a way to save them and a regular time to look at them. There are more than you think.
4. Wear your version of a power suit. The way we dress is a good way to show respect, but it can also be a celebration. Typically, my business

clients want to feel in control, on top of things, successful, and accomplished. Celebrate all of the things you have done by wearing something that makes you feel that way. It can be a power tie, boots, a suit, a slick belt. Whatever makes you feel that swagger.

5. Track progress. That may not sound like a celebration, but tally marks, notes, stars, whatever tracks the effort you are putting in gives you a visual reminder and can feel great. I have a client who bought a Lego trophy kit. Each Step his team gets closer to their sales goal, he adds Legos.

6. Go high. A lot of football teams have a sign above a doorway and they each hit it as they walk out the locker room door. You can do this at work. You can put a sign, a note, or even a tiny sticker above the door to your office then stretch up to touch it every time you do something (have a great sales call, finish a tax return, sign up a new client).

7. Beautify your space. It can mean rearranging the layout so you have a better view, adding photos or tapestries, or removing extra furniture, files, or other junk. My mother used to buy a bouquet of flowers from the corner vendor every Monday. She would keep them at her desk all week to enjoy.

8. Change your password. I type in my password many times a day, so it's a great opportunity to choose something I like. Next time you achieve something, you can change it to "Ididit456$" or "W1nneroftheaward" (come up with your own)

9. Light it up. I knew a couple who were serious hockey fans. They had a hockey goal light just like the ones that light up when a goal is scored in the NHL. You can get a hockey light, a bell to ring, a horn to squawk, and turn it on when you want to celebrate.

10. Install a kegerator. It's a fridge meant to hold a keg of beer. I worked in an office that had one, locked away, and we would celebrate with a 5pm beer sometimes. If that's not appropriate or desirable, can you install something else fun? Cold brew on tap, a putting green.

10 Ways to Celebrate in the Buff

I didn't know if I should include this list. But the purpose of this chapter is to help you think of ideas you might not otherwise consider. We all have bodies, so it's likely at least a couple of these will work for you. No one has to know.

1. Take a bath. Use bubbles or a bomb or oil. Bring a beer, whiskey, cold water, juice, seltzer. Play music, light a candle, whatever you like. This is not gender specific.
2. Sing in the shower. Belt out any song you know or make one up.
3. Flex your muscles in front of the mirror and say something nice to yourself. Don't have muscles? Admire your gorgeous hair or smooth bald head.
4. Have relations with yourself. I don't think I need to add any explanation to this one.
5. Take off your socks and put your bare feet directly into the soft grass. If only your feet are in the buff for this, you can do it at the park, soccer field, anywhere. But if you have a nice lawn and a privacy fence...
6. Put sliced cucumber on your eyes. It's cool and soothing and forces you to close your eyes and relax for a minute. Do it with as many or few clothes on as you'd like. You can also use a metal spoon or an ice cube.
7. Write yourself a smiley face or happy note in the steam on the mirror when you get out of the shower. Next time it steams, the note or face will show up again to make you happy.

8. Sleep. Next time you have fresh sheets on your bed, sleep in the buff. Spread out and take the whole bed if you can. (You can keep a robe nearby if you're worried a fire will erupt in the middle of the night.)

9. Get a spray tan. We all know the sun is dangerous, but for some of us that golden glow feels amazing. You can go to a booth or have a professional spray you.

10. Float. Look up float tanks, also called sensory deprivation tanks. They are filled with salt water so you float, in privacy, in a pod or a tub. It's incredibly relaxing. And many are large so you won't feel claustrophobic.

10 Ways to Celebrate Based on Your Love Language

If you are unfamiliar with the love languages or just don't know yours, look up: 5lovelanguages.com
The five love languages each have two suggestions below. Remember that all of these celebrations are meant for you to do for yourself. So while the love languages are how you like to receive love, I believe that you can find ways to offer all 5 of them to yourself.

1. Words of Affirmation: Take the joy you feel in the moment and write a note to your future self. Tell future you all of the reasons you are awesome and hide the note somewhere you will find it later or mail it to yourself.
2. Words of Affirmation: Post words that you love somewhere. In a frame, on a white board, above a workbench in the garage, on a tattoo on your arm.
3. Quality Time: Set aside a celebration hour once a week where you will spend time with yourself and reflect on the steps you have taken.
4. Quality Time: Sit and spend time with a loved one. A family member, pet, neighbor.
5. Physical Touch: Schedule a massage, haircut, shave, or any other physical treat.
6. Physical Touch: Use something that feels good. This could be a cashmere blanket, a fragrant lotion, a crisply ironed shirt, just resting your hand over your heart.

7. Acts of Service: Hire someone to do something for you, and then really enjoy it. Whether it's a gardener, travel agent, grocery delivery, let someone take something off of your list.

8. Acts of Service: Can you do something ahead of time for yourself? Double your recipe and freeze half so you have dinner next week. Set the coffee pot up to be ready the night before. Put gas in your car tonight so you don't have to do it in the morning.

9. Receiving Gifts: Subscribe to a monthly subscription box, and each month a surprise will show up at your door. It can be shaving supplies, crafts, beauty, beef, toys, t-shirts. The types of boxes are endless.

10. Receiving Gifts: Next time you order something for yourself on-line, use the giftwrap feature. You can have it wrapped and sent to your own address.

10 Ways to Celebrate That are Over the Top

We're trying to make celebration accessible, easy, and a regular habit. But sometimes you need to think big. Now that we've thought of small, simple, or frugal ways to celebrate, here are some over the top ideas.

1. Get a chocolate fountain. You can rent one, buy one, or find a restaurant that features one. This could instead be a champagne fountain, a cheese fountain, or maybe you can invent a new fountain request.
2. Drive to Vegas. Or drive anywhere fun you can get within a few hours. Drive to a big city, a beach town, an amusement park. Take a road trip and don't come back for at least two days.
3. Get really dressed up. Put on your black-tie attire. Rent a tuxedo or a gown if you have to and go anywhere. Go bowling, or to the Waffle House, or the Opera. You'll feel like a big deal. Bonus points for adding a corsage, boutonniere, or other prom-like accessory.
4. Rent a car. What kind of car have you always wanted to drive? A convertible? A huge SUV? A tiny sports car? Rent one just for the day and take a little drive. You can go up the coast, through the drive through, to the mountains, to pick up carpool.
5. Buy something blingy. It doesn't have to be worthy of wearing to the Oscars. I bought myself a goddess necklace as a celebration and it really does make me feel like a goddess.

It can be a watch, including an activity tracker watch, if that's more your speed. As long as it feels like a celebration.

6. Make a big donation. It can be anonymous or fully identified. A big donation might be $20, $100, $1,000, $50,000, it all depends on your budget and perspective. Who do you want to support? Is there a national organization? A local school group? A hotline, shelter, cause in your community?

7. Get a tattoo. Something small and special or huge and bold. A family member who beat cancer got a tattoo to celebrate. Several people I know celebrated the birth of a child by getting a tattoo. You can also order specialty temporary tattoos with your business logo and give those out.

8. Buy a plane ticket. Is there a fun place or person you'd like to visit? Go for a quick weekend. Disneyland, Atlantic City, your aunt in Texas, college roommate in Indiana, New York City, Denver, New Orleans. Just pack up and go without overthinking.

9. Jump out of an airplane. Not the plane you caught above, but actually sign up for sky-diving. So many people have this on their bucket list. Do it now.

10. Hire a driver. This can be a limousine or town car, a party bus, a helicopter...

CONCLUSION – LET'S CELEBRATE TOGETHER

I've said here that you can celebrate by yourself without permission or approval from anyone else.

That doesn't mean you HAVE to celebrate alone. My coaching philosophy is that positive change for yourself is easier when it's not by yourself. So let's celebrate together.

I'd love to hear from you if you've celebrated using any of the suggestions in this book. Even better, if you have your own celebration that you're willing to share, I'd love to hear that. I'm always looking for ideas on how to celebrate. Email me at tommiejean@tommiejean.com

And if you feel stuck trying to figure out what steps you should be celebrating, coaching can help. This is your invitation to join me as a coaching client. To find out more, see: tommiejean.com

ACKNOWLEDGEMENTS

Thank you to the lovely ladies in the OT6 morning accountability group who inspired this topic: Alison, Amy, Colleen, Elena, Marianne, and Samantha. And thank you to Susan for bringing us all together.

Thanks to Joe for believing in me from the earliest days of my coaching journey. Thank you to Eric for your encouragement and unwavering excitement about my coaching and this book.

Thank you to Alison and Gabe for the editing and reviews and the encouragement. Thank you to Laci for pushing me to commit to a date and get it done, and for helping me tell the world about it. Speaking of Get it Done, thank you to Alex Franzen for showing so many of us that the books inside of us can become reality.

Thank you to Maggie and Abby, two little girls with big hearts who are always as proud of me as I am of them. And thank you to my extended family, near and far – Winklers, Romanos, Larys, Franks, Lindseys, Damrels, Boscheinens, Chases, Cleggs, and all the rest. Having family to celebrate with is .

Thank you to Chauna and Christen who both literally picked me up off the floor during my lowest point. We would all give each other the shirt off our backs, the shoes off our feet, the strength to go on. I love you so much.

Thanks to Cory, Rhea, and Esperanza because you ladies have celebrated laughter and tears, ups and downs, holidays and weekdays by my side.

And thank you to all of my coaching clients for sharing your goals, your struggles, and your wins with me.

ABOUT THE AUTHOR

Tommie Jean is a coach for small business owners and entrepreneurs. The great thing about Tommie Jean: she doesn't care what you do. Find your own path, the goals that light you up, and the crazy ideas that you just can't let go of. She wants to help you reach your goals, whatever they are.

Tommie Jean lives in Northern California with her daughter Magnolia. The purpose of her life is to joyfully create.

Made in United States
North Haven, CT
03 September 2022